THE
POWER
OF
TITHING
$$$$$

(The book the enemy does not want you to read)

SARAH C.A. BALLARD

The Power Of Tithing $$$$

© 2022 Sarah C.A. Ballard

ISBN 978-1-66783-637-9

eBook ISBN 978-1-66783-638-6

TABLE OF CONTENTS

DEDICATION

To my husband, Brigadier General Retired
Edward H. Ballard, with all my love.

SPECIAL THANKS

To our wonderful son, Alexander Nathaniel Ballard, and his lovely wife, Alexandria Gabrielle Ballard. I accepted Jesus as my personal Savior while I was pregnant with Alexander. I got baptized and received the gift of the Holy Ghost a year later. God often used Alex to pull me to Jesus throughout my early years in Him.

To Dr. Aquilla Rice, Bernadette Ballard, Master Sergeant (Retired) William Ballard, and my entire family. It is interesting how whenever you need them, family is always there. Family never lets you down. Even with the many twists and turns of life, we can always depend on my family.

To my spiritual father, Apostle Franklin Cornelius Showell. His guidance and overseeing while completing New Life, Temple Life, the W.A. Showell School of Ministry, and the Eldership Catechism and Training Course taught me how to serve the Lord. Apostle's many messages preached repeatedly encouraged me, and helped me to press on in my walk with Jesus.

To First Lady Ella Augusta Showell, who requested that I assist with a particular project that led me right back to sitting in front of my laptop, typing away! Her love and caring over the years kept me focused on this book. First Lady and I often have fun working on various projects. I especially thank God for the many times that she and I have laughed together.

To Bishop Carolyn Showell for her many prayers while serving as her adjutant.

To Dr. Leonard Raucher, the most skilled physician I have ever known. He kept me on target with my physicals and other healthcare needs without being too pushy. This aspect of his medical care is wonderful.

FOREWARD

The scriptures advise every believer to commit a tenth of all they have to the Lord, and to set it aside as holy unto Him. We don't just tithe out of duty to God but out of our vast love for Him and the many blessings he has bestowed upon us. Over my many years as pastor of First Apostolic Faith Church, I have taught numerous theological courses, and preached more sermons than I can count on tithing as a key cornerstone in the life of the believer. Yet tithing remains a challenge we must learn to embrace with a cheerful heart.

Tithing is a discipline that doesn't come easy for some, especially during times of economic hardship and struggle. And even though God promises to provide all of our needs when we commit to giving of our first fruits, many Christians choose fear over faith. When we refuse to give unto God, the scripture calls it robbery. We, as saints, are called to build God's kingdom, not steal from it.

In this book, Elder Ballard makes the valiant attempt to bridge the gap between God's directive to tithe and the believer's heart to follow God's plan.

I pray that the words in this book will resonate with anyone who wants to make tithing a consistent priority in their lives. It is my hope that this book will be more than a guide to understand tithing as just an act of obedience. May it open your eyes to tithing as an act of worship to the Almighty.

Apostle Franklin C. Showell

Senior Pastor, First Apostolic Faith Church of Jesus Christ International, Inc.

ACKNOWLEDGEMENT

Several years ago when my sister passed away, I believe that it was at this point that Pastor Kimberly Showell began praying for me. She never mentioned this to me, but I believe this was the starting point of her prayers. Pastor Kimberly serves as the Administrative Pastor for our church, The First Apostolic Faith Church of Jesus Christ International, Incorporated. While I believe that she is in constant prayer for many members of our church, I know that God used Pastor Kimberly in my life. I can never thank her enough for her many prayers and hours of listening when needed. She is a great example of a Godly woman who sincerely cares about the needs of the members of First Apostolic, and that we each reach our full potential in God.

PREFACE

Tithe –

1. One tenth

2. Tenth of money or possessions

3. To tithe is to give of one's money to **GOD**

4. Tithing is a way to worship and obey God

5. To fail to tithe is to rob God

CHAPTER 1
"TITHING – BORING."

"Will a man rob God? Yet ye have robbed me. But ye say, Wherein have we robbed thee? In tithes and offerings... Bring ye all the tithes into the storehouse..." Malachi 3:8-10.

The Bible is the inspired Word of God. The Holy Scripture of the Bible is made up of thirty-nine Old Testament books, and twenty-seven New Testament books. The New Testament was originally written in Greek. Written originally in Hebrew, the Old Testament is divided into the five books of Law, History, Poetry, Major Prophets and Minor Prophets. The sermons of this Old Testament prophet gives us the Book of Malachi, categorized as one of the Minor Prophets. The book is considered a minor prophetical book not because it is less important than the major prophetical books, but because the book is somewhat short when compared to longer books written by the prophets. Written to the Israelites, its main theme focuses on final warnings, the sin of Israel, and God's judgement. The name Malachi means messenger. Seeing the people backslide into their old habits of sin, Malachi rebukes them for their present spiritual condition. Malachi also examines the faithfulness of the priests and people of Israel, and predicts the coming of the Messiah.

But why you may ask write a book about tithing? How boring can that be? Most people know about tithing, how much to tithe, and the importance of tithing. Tithing is often an area where many people claim to differ in opinions. Many say, "Why should I pay the church my hard earned money?" Is it the love of money that makes it challenging for us to tithe?

Years ago .....

As a result of this Word from the Lord, I have continued to write. I took a break from writing for about a year after a very bad incident with a publisher. This particular publisher unfortunately got me for $500. While I tried to pursue receiving a refund from this particular publisher, I never recovered the $500. All I can say at this point is "Please have mercy Lord". "But whoso shall offend one of these little ones which believe in me, it were better for him that a millstone were hanged about his neck, and that he were drowned in the depth of the sea. Woe unto the world because of offences! For it must needs be that offences come; but woe to that man by whom the offence cometh! (Matthew 18:6-7).

However after taking a break from writing for about a year, I felt that the Lord was encouraging me to write again. I can only assume that the possible publisher of my previous book missed an awesome opportunity for like this book, I cannot take any credit for the previous book that I was about to publish. *God* gave me the words for my previous book, therefore that publisher would have sold millions of copies. And while tithing is not a popular topic, this book in the Name of Jesus will sell in the millions because this writing is God's Words, not mine. *"God* did it" (Apostle Cornelius Showell). To God be the glory!

So why would God lay it on my heart to write about tithing? Is it possible that tithing is one of the most effective forms of Spiritual Warfare? God actually gave me another book idea but I selected this topic from God for now. (Thank you Jesus)! Honestly, one of the reasons that I went with this topic is that I have a feeling that the enemy does not like it when we tithe. So I am thinking that any topic that is contrary to satan's plan must be a best seller! But I also noticed a financial struggle within my family, among my friends, even some of my colleagues in the workplace were struggling financially. I wondered if one of the reasons for their financial problems was due to their lack of tithing, or lack of tithing consistently. I wonder if some of the back-biting and clawing our way to the top in our workforce would even be considered if employees simply tithed? Would companies need to close their businesses if the owners paid tithes to the Lord? If the owners tithed could their companies stay open instead of closing? Offerings are crucial as well. Malachi mentions both tithes and offerings in verse eight. But I'm curious as to why Malachi comes back in verse ten and mentions the tithe yet again. Is it possible that God was using Brother Malachi to place more emphasis on the tithe? Is it possible that God mentions tithing more because the tithe is often a larger portion of our income than the offering thereby making the paying of the tithe a bit more challenging than giving offerings? Could it be that the tithe is a more consistent giving because the Bible gives a directive describing the exact amount that should be paid for the tithe? Please don't get it twisted; I am not minimizing the offering. Malachi tells us that we unfortunately rob the Lord in both tithes *and* offerings. While I have not done research (yet) regarding this next statement that I am about to make, I suspect that most people who attend church on a regular basis are doing ok with paying offerings. But I also suspect that most people who attend church regularly are failing miserably with paying their tithes. Even the location of the book within the Old Testament is interesting. There are certain books that are so easy to find in the Bible. You know how it is when the speaker asks you to turn in your Bible to the text from which the preacher is about to preach. Those who have memorized where all the books of the Bible are located have no problem at all turning straight to the needed verse. But most of us still fumble a bit or have to give it a bit of thought as to the exact location of the text. Yet there are some books that are extremely easy to locate. Genesis, being at the beginning is super easy. The book of Psalms located midway of the Bible is not too challenging. The splendid location of Revelation at the end of our Bibles presents no challenge even to a new believer. And Malachi is pretty conveniently located as well, as most of us know approximately where the New Testament begins in our Bibles, so Malachi is just before the New

Testament. It is almost as if the Lord wanted to prevent any excuse for not being able to get to this particular book, the book of Malachi.

CHAPTER 2
MALACHI

So who was Malachi? What do we know about him? Brother Malachi was an Old Testament prophet whose messages produced the Book of Malachi. Among the Minor Prophets, we really do not hear much about Malachi. Yet this particular verse is the topic of many discussions today. And this particular verse is a part of the lives of many believers today. Malachi 3:8-10 is plastered on the tithe and offering envelopes of millions of churches all across the globe. How wonderful that God can use a teeny, tiny book with only four chapters to positively affect the lives of so many. How amazing that the Lord can take one sentence out of a teeny, tiny book to enrich the lives of believers all across the world!

Again, the name "Malachi" means messenger. And Brother Malachi still relays his very important messages to us even today. How many messages have we heard preached about the importance of tithing? Yet after hearing sermon after sermon, and message after message after message, we often completely refuse to tithe. Or very similar to dieting, we make a commitment to consistently tithe. But somehow get off track. Then we wonder why our credit card balances are so high. Or even worse we struggle to make ends meet when paying our bills. We give to this organization or that organization, when God clearly tells us to bring the tithes into the store house meaning the church. The Bible does not say to bring the tithes to this or that organization. The Lord says "the storehouse" meaning God's house, the church. Tithing must become a way of life. A wise elder once taught us that "tithing is a principle" (Pitts, Kevin, 2005). You can never go wrong by paying your tithes. Only good things, primarily financial blessings, are produced by tithing.

Speaking in approximately 450 B.C., Malachi questions the people and priests regarding their unfaithfulness. It is quite interesting that faith, or lack thereof was a prominent discussion from Malachi. Faith is directly tied to the tithe. "Now faith is the substance of things hoped for..." (Hebrews 11:1). Just as Malachi preached about having faith to honor God in the days of old, so do our current preachers speak of having faith to honor God with our tithes. It is a difficult concept to grasp. How can one think that paying out more cash can in fact increase your cash flow? One tends to think that by hoarding your cash in your bank account, your bank account will grow. All I can tell you here is, "try it." If you have been an inconsistent tither, the only way that you will know that this principle works is to simply try it. I guarantee you that He will "open you the windows of heaven, and pour you out a blessing" (Malachi 3:10). But here's the thing, Malachi takes it a step further. He says that not only will God pour you out a blessing, God will do this in a manner that "there shall not shall be room enough for you to receive it." Can you imagine that?

Many scholars date this writing during the rule of Xerxes I because of the discussion of a governor. Several commentators date the book of Malachi during the early Persian period between the restoration of the second Temple in 515 B.C. and Nehemiah's mission in 445 B.C. (Achtemeier, 1985, The HarperCollins Bible Dictionary). Since Malachi served at the time of Nehemiah, it is assumed that Malachi also lived in Jerusalem.

CHAPTER 3

MALACHI 3:7-8

Now that we have a bit of background about Malachi, let's examine this most important scripture about tithing. Let's back up to verse seven, before Malachi directly addresses tithing. Here Malachi talks to the people about how "from the days of their fathers" the people have strayed away from the Lord's ordinances. An ordinance can be defined as an authoritative decree or direction. So the Lord tells the people through Brother Malachi that they have strayed away from God's decree, and have not kept God's decree. Sound familiar? The Lord goes onto to tell the people to "Return unto me'" and by doing this God promises to return to the people. This theme should also be familiar. But God takes it a step further because He is God, so he knows everything. So God realizes that the people may ask, "Wherein shall we return"? Another way of stating this is that the people may ask, "How shall we return unto you Lord"? The Lord in His infinite wisdom answers the question with a question. He asks if a man will rob God. The all-knowing God knows again what the people will ask. He knows the people will ask how they have robbed God. This time the Lord does not answer this question with a question. He instead gives a blunt, easily understandable answer. The Lord through Malachi tells the people that they have robbed Him through their tithes and offerings.

This discussion from the Lord brings up two extremely important points from verses seven and eight. One, please note that the Lord is saying that if you feel that you have turned away from God's decrees, specifically the decree where God commands that we tithe, one way to return to God and to keep his decree is to *simply tithe*. We've all been there, right? I do not think that there is even one believer who really loves the Lord, and still, at some point during their Holy Ghost filled life with God, does not get off track with tithing. Let's be honest. Whether this experience occurred when you first came to know the Lord and struggled a bit with tithing. Whether you have known the Lord for years and decided at some point to spend more money in another area instead of paying your tithes. Or maybe you have been saved for decades and unfortunately got off track with paying your tithes in error. The important point to note here is that God considers this error as "going away from his ordinance or direction." Tithing is a serious matter. Just as robbing a convenience store is in fact breaking an ordinance or law, robbing God by not tithing is breaking an ordinance of the Almighty. An even more serious offense, than robbing a convenience store, especially when we know better, when we already know that it is the right thing to do to tithe, and most importantly when we see who it is that we are robbing regarding the tithe . Similarly in Nehemiah 13:11 the question is asked, "Why is the house of God neglected"? Verses seven and eight indicate that when we do not tithe we have committed a double sin:

1. we have gone away from God's ordinances

2. also, we have robbed God

Most of us would not even consider robbing a convenience store, a grocery store or an individual. Yet the reality is that month after month, many believers consistently rob God by not tithing!

CHAPTER 4
MALACHI 3:9A

"Ye are cursed with a curse". Wow, I would not want to be the recipient of this verse. But I believe that I have been the recipient in the past. I was baptized in 1991, and received the precious gift of the Holy Ghost the following year at the age of 33. I was what the saints often refer to as a "pew baby". My mom took my sister and me to church EVERY Sunday. But my mom had not received the Holy Ghost when I was young. I really do not know if she was a consistent tither when I was young. I praise my mom for being a wonderful mom. She was a hard worker. And while she may not have had a personal relationship with the Lord when I was younger, she clearly knew of God. She took great care of me and my sister. She did her very best to provide for us. Thank God later in life my mom received the Holy Ghost and became an extremely consistent tither. But this was when I no longer lived with her. So I missed the opportunity to see the benefits received by a consistent tither as a child. While I remember the passing of the plate during offering time in church, this is the only memory that I have regarding giving from my *childhood*. I received no formal instructions regarding tithing from my mom as a child.

I was told who my biological parents were at the age of eleven. I commend my birth parents for doing exactly what the mother of Moses did for him. To spare his life, she put him on the river to be found and raised by the daughter of Pharaoh. To spare my life for they could have aborted me, my birth parents sent me to be raised by my great aunt. Abortion is a sin, I am sure of this. Some people think that if you terminate a pregnancy very early on, that it is not considered murder. This is not scriptural. I literally know the day that my husband and I conceived our son. Often only a woman who has carried a child can understand this statement. And so I say to our young people who have not murdered their babies, God will bless you, for you have chosen to do the right thing by not killing your child. Abortion is a very serious matter! However the best way to prevent children out of wedlock is to not have sex. Yes, many methods of birth control are effective. But I do not recall any being 100% effective except for abstinence. Yes, there are tons of birth control methods available, but I just do not recall reading about any of these popular forms of birth control in the Bible. However I do recall reading that fornication which is sexual intercourse between people who are not married is a sin – that's in the Bible. I feel so sorry for our young people today because, similar to my generation, they are often *encouraged* to have sex before marriage. We [parents] try to teach them to wait, but peer pressure in high school may override the advice that our young people receive from their parents. And if we are able to get them to wait until they go off to college, then they get the freedom to have sex on college campuses which is not the reason that they are attending college. Universities teach that the fetus is not viable until a certain time. And our young people fall for this statement because they can use this excuse to rationalize aborting a baby. Only to find later in life that the university professors were wrong. My aunt used to say, "You are the company that you keep", (Alaba, Dorothy). If you hang out with people who believe in abortion, you may end up aborting a baby. If you hang out with people who fornicate, the subject will come up repeatedly and the next thing you know, you are having premarital sex. Many young people have been raised in the church before they go off to college. Mom and Dad cannot be with our young people 24 hours a day. Our young people know right from wrong. The question is, do they *really want* to be kept? Do they really *want* to live Holy? Just as we as adults have to be very careful about our friends, so our young people must do the same. *If* you *really* want to live for Jesus, be careful about the company that you keep. Be careful who you hang out with. Be careful about what you allow your eyes to see and your ears to hear. Make a conscious commitment to live for Christ!

Oops, let me get back on track to the subject of Malachi. I do not recall ever missing church up until the age of approximately 13. As a teenager, I could have gone to church with my grandmother. But I did not choose to press my way. I could have pressed my way to church and received a first-hand experience with my grandmother regarding the importance of tithing. Therefore, similar to my childhood years, as a teenager I had no close example or formal teaching regarding tithing.

As I entered my twenties I still did not pursue a relationship with God. I attended church periodically. And while our church leaders do an outstanding job teaching the importance of tithing, because I knew *of* God, instead of really knowing God, I dismissed what I did hear about giving when I attended church. So again, similar to my childhood and teen years, with no one in my life to whom I was close to set the example of being a tither, I chose not to tithe.

While I was on bedrest pregnant with our son, I began reading my Bible. I also began watching Christian television remembering that as an adult when I went to visit my mom, she often had the channel turned to a Christian station. I gave my life to the Lord in our living room one day when I was pregnant with our son while I was watching Christian TV.

I realized when our son was a newborn that there was no way that I could raise him without God in his life. But how could I teach our son if I did not *really* know the Lord? So after the birth of our son, I began coming to church consistently. I would often sit with my sister and my niece. I noticed that my sister would constantly give, she was a consistent tither. One day, I was about to go to the table to give my offering. My sister asked me to take her tithe and offering up to the offering table for her. I knew that what I was about to do was wrong, but I did it anyway. After my sister placed her envelopes in my hand, I looked at the amount that my sister wrote on her tithe envelope that showed what she was giving. I was so shocked at the astronomical amount that my sister was giving that immediately I looked at her and asked, "You are giving this much"? She looked me right in the eye and replied, "Indeed I am". I believe that this was the first teaching that I *experienced* about tithing. I believe that my sister was hoping that I would look down at her envelope so that she could use this as a teaching moment. My sister did not tell me to tithe. I had already heard that periodically when I was in my twenties. She did not preach to me the importance of tithing. The preachers and speakers had already done this as I was now attending church consistently. No, instead my sister literally showed me how to tithe! She did not just "talk the talk"; she "walked the walk". You see, I knew that God had already blessed my sister with a good job, a wonderful family, a beautiful home, and a fair amount of pocket change. It was rare that she lacked financially. I already knew that my sister was doing well. So when I saw the amount that she tithed, I easily made that connection between tithing and being financially blessed. I understood first-hand the benefits of tithing.

I pray that I have not bored you with a summary of my childhood. But I write this section to discuss an extremely important point. Parents, the church does so much to help our children, to teach our children. But as parents, it is our responsibility to teach our children to tithe. This can be a challenge if you are unequally yoked. But we must ask God to help us to teach our children to tithe. Like me, if we do not teach them in their childhood, their teens, or even their twenties they will not know the importance of tithing. The enemy loves it when we do not teach our children the tithing principle. The scripture says, "...and pour you out a blessing, that there shall not be room enough to receive it". Please forgive me parents if this next statement is a bit harsh. But parents, how many blessings have not been poured out to our children because we did not teach them the importance of tithing? I vaguely recall that my sister taught my niece to tithe when my niece was in her teens. With her first little part-time job selling snow balls at the corner store, my niece began tithing. She has been a consistent tither ever since. My niece Melissa is now happily married, she has a very successful career, and most importantly, she and I received the gift of the Holy Ghost on the same day! I believe the Lord has in fact "poured [Melissa] out a blessing that there shall not be room enough to receive it". Parents, we do not want our children to be "cursed with a curse". Therefore if we want blessings poured out on our children that they do not have room enough to receive, we must teach our children to tithe! It is easier to do this if we start as early as possible as we bring them to church even as toddlers and teach them to give on Sundays. And teach them to give even as children.

CHAPTER 5
MALACHI 3:9B

"...for ye have robbed me, even this whole nation". We have already analyzed the suggestion that robbing anyone is not a good thing. And we have discussed how robbing God is even worse. I pray this sentence of the scripture is settled and clear in our minds at this point. I have read this scripture several times over the past few years. We've all seen it on contribution envelopes and heard this text preached on various occasions. But I seemed to miss the last part of the "b" portion of the text, "even this whole nation". Let's see what the Bible says about this phrase.

Readers, please forgive me if this next statement that I will make offends you. But I must admit that, another one of the reasons that I wrote this book is that, while African Americans have made great strides during my life time: we've had an African American president, we see more African American physicians, dentists and professionals now more than ever, even more African American CEO's. But it seems that as a people, we still lack a great deal financially. I realize that part of the reason for our financial plight may be due to lack of education and poor parenting as a result of fornication producing teenage pregnancy. But I can't help but wonder if this "whole nation" concept mentioned by Malachi has something to do with our lack of tithing as a people. Let's turn to the New International Version (NIV) of the Bible for clarity for this section.

Verse nine of the NIV reads "You are under a curse – the whole nation of you – because of robbing me". A nation can be defined as a "large political division, normally of a homogenous ethnic population" (Achtemeier, 1985,

p. 741). Based on this definition the African American population could be considered a nation. So if we re-write Brother Malachi's verse 9 could we possibly say, "...for African Americans have robbed God, even the whole African American nation"? The Bible teaches us to help one another. And I know of several family members (one in particular) who seems to always be there to lend a helping hand financially to others. But is it possible that we as a nation are not doing enough to help ourselves? If only 30% of family members in each family are tithing, would this be considered robbing God? If only 30% of the African American race are tithing, would this constitute Brother Malachi's definition of the whole African American nation robbing God? Please don't get me wrong, I love our people. But I still wonder if we had more consistent tithers within our race, would we then be so blessed as a people that there is not even room enough for us to receive blessings as a *people*? Is it possible that one of the reasons that our Jewish sisters and brothers are so blessed is because of their faithful and consistent tithing?

CHAPTER 6
MALACHI 3:10

We have already examined the importance of bringing tithes into the storehouse to the Lord. I think that we are clear on this point. We have also discussed the statement that the Lord will "open you the windows of heaven, and pour you out a blessing, that there shall not be room enough to receive it". I believe we are clear regarding this point as well. Now we will explore two more phrases within this verse:

1. "... that there may be meat in mine house..."

2. "... and prove me now herewith..."

1. While many have decreased the amount of meat in their diets in more recent years, studies show that not just some, but all of the nutrients and essential amino acids that our bodies need can be obtained by meat consumption. One extremely popular substance in today's diets is protein. This can also be provided by eating meat. B12 is a natural vitamin contained in meat. And here's a fact that I was surprised to discover: weight loss and weight management can be acquired by including meat as a major source of our food plan. Even the processed meats that we find so convenient are packed with iron, zinc and other vitamins and minerals that our bodies need.

But with all the *hoopla* about this tasty treat, one can actually survive without meat. In the days of old, "Meat was also a part of the diet, but for the ordinary Israelite only on special occasions, since it was too expensive for daily fare". (Achtemeier, 1985, p.

345). So we see here that meat is not needed to survive, and it is pricy to consume meat on a daily basis. But Malachi says that after we bring all the tithes to the Lord, there will be this rich, extra, delicacy of an item which is not needed for our survival in our homes. Is it possible that the Lord was saying through Brother Malachi that by tithing, we will not only survive, but we will experience the riches, the extras, the delicacies of life? He already said He would supply our every need. But is it possible that by tithing we experience the exceeding abundant life?

2. I have only been saved about 30 years. I still have so much to learn about the Lord, and I am still learning. But I do not recall often hearing the Lord asking us to "prove Him". This phrase really caught my attention because most believers reverence God. We set Him on a high throne, He is set above all things. And while Jesus came humbly as a lamb, He is still a great king, high and lifted up. But I get the feeling

from this phrase, "prove Him" that this is one of the few exceptions where He is trying to relate to us one on one. It is almost as if He is saying, "Yes, I am your king. But regarding tithing, I want you to know that I am really here for you." It is almost as if the Lord knew that tithing might be challenging for us, and He needs us to know that He will come through. So much so that He literally challenges us in this area. It is almost as if Jesus is saying, "I dare you to use the faith of the grain of a mustard seed and tithe, and watch what I do"!

In 2017 I gave a testimony in church regarding proving God. What had happened was☺, I was serving as an adjutant for the First Lady of our church. As a result of serving, I decided to attend our Church Anniversary services on the nights that *she* attended. Our church lists several of our members on teams for these nightly services. However if you are not listed on a team, you get the opportunity to ask to be a member of someone's team. This is a wonderful exchange because, the person that you ask is often so extremely honored that you asked to be on their team. And you are so excited when they answer "yes". This team concept also builds unity among team members.

For 2017, I was not listed with a team. I decided that since I was serving our First Lady, it would be easiest to simply contribute to her team. I wrote the check for the Church Anniversary on a Monday. I put the check in my purse because the Church Anniversary night for our team was not until Thursday. But by Tuesday, an unexpected check arrived in the mail for me. I had not even delivered the check to the Lord at church yet. But the Lord delivered a check to me! His Word says "prove me". I believe this is a perfect example that God will ALWAYS prove Himself to be true to His word. When we give, He will open up the windows of heaven and pour us out a blessing. This check was clearly a check that I did not have room enough to receive. I did not even know that the check was coming!

I mentioned earlier how even "seasoned saints" can get a bit off track with tithing. There is no excuse for this, but I believe if we would all be honest we would have to say that it happens. Even if it was only once during our saved lives, it happens. This happened to me during a time when I was extremely busy. Once I got my act together, I implemented a procedure to prevent this from happening in the future. You may want to try this since it really helps me. I know the millennials may not use check books anymore. But my generation may still use check books as a tool to keep an eye on our balance. However the concept will work for young people as well. Most of us get paid on a regular basis through our employers. This might be weekly, bi-weekly, or monthly. Depending on the time that we receive our paychecks, we may not have time to pay our bills. We may need to put bill paying off to another day, even if we do it electronically. But what I began doing is not writing my tithe check when I pay my bills. Instead, I now write out my tithe check the minute that I record my paycheck. I am so dedicated to follow the ordinance of the Lord, and not rob God, that I even use a different color ink (red) in my checkbook. I record my deposit from my employer, but the very next line in my checkbook under my deposit is the check for my tithes. This not only forces me to pay it right away, but every now and then if I get the least bit concerned that I did not pay my tithes, the deposit and the check amount are written right there together, in red. There is never a question that the tithe was not paid if I need to double check.

After only about 2 months of implementing this procedure, a funny thing happened. I recorded my *regular pay* deposit, then wrote and recorded my tithe check. Please keep in mind that again, I "wrote the check". Later I called my bank to confirm my deposit. There was an ADDITIONAL deposit in my account. My employer had paid a bonus that I did not know about. But here's the interesting part. I've heard people say that God has a sense of humor. After this incident, I am inclined to agree with them. This was another situation where I simply "wrote the check," had not delivered the check to the Lord yet, and already the Lord "proved Himself" by delivering additional monies to my account. Oh but there's more, I still laugh when I think about this now because I know, this *had* to be God. The amount in dollars of the bonus that the Lord delivered to my checking account, was the EXACT SAME AMOUNT of the tithe check that I had just written but not yet delivered to church! There is no way that this could be a coincidence. That's the Lord proving Himself. He says "prove me"!

Of course with so many electronic methods now available, consistent tithing is effortless.

CHAPTER 7

MALACHI 3:11

"And I will rebuke the devourer for your sakes." Could this possibly mean that for the tither, for those that tithe, God will correct the destroyer, or enemy for those that tithe? In other words, is it possible that tithers do not have to worry about our enemies because God will handle them, take care of them, correct them, and disapprove them? "For the battle is not yours, but God's" (2 Chron20:15).

"...and he shall not destroy the fruits of your ground..." The term fruit can represent many things. Fruit can be defined as the fruit of the womb, or our children. Fruit can also be defined as our earnings or paychecks. But in this passage as is the case with so many biblical references in the Word of God, Brother Malachi is referring to agriculture, literally meaning actual fruit often produced directly or indirectly from the ground. And so again

God is saying that for the tither, for those that tithe, the destroyer AKA satan, shall not destroy the fruit AKA your paycheck. How wonderful is that? Isn't it wonderful to know that by simply tithing the enemy cannot destroy your earnings? In light of mergers, acquisitions, restructurings and now even government lay-offs, simply tithing can defeat all of that! "Consider the lilies of the field!" (Matt. 6:28).

"Neither shall your vine cast her fruit before the time in the field." Please keep in mind who is speaking here. Chapter one, verse one explains that the book of Malachi is the "... word of the Lord..." Also, please keep in mind that Brother Malachi was a prophet. A vine is a "creeping or climbing plant that produces grapes (or melons or cucumbers)." I wonder what a grape that is produced in a field before it's time, before it has time to mature, looks like, tastes like. Just imagine for a moment, a grape produced by a grapevine at the right time in the field. I would assume that this grape would be extremely sweet, almost perfect. Conversely, imagine a grape produced by a grapevine "before the time in the field." I can only assume that this grape would be bitter, virtually imperfect. We want our vines to carry our fruit until they are fully ripe. We want the fruit that we produce with the help of the Lord to be completely mature. How can we truly and sincerely display love, joy, peace, longsuffering, gentleness, goodness, faith, meekness, and temperance without spiritual maturity? Did the Lord reveal to the prophet that simply tithing will prevent the abortion of the fruit of the Spirit in those individuals that tithe?

Malachi 3:12

Like many believers, I am guilty of using biblical terms without knowing the true definition of the word. For example when we use the term "blessed," we often think of financial prosperity. However the proper definition of blessed is "Made happy by God." We know this must be true when we see headlines about celebrities who had tons of money but were so unhappy that they turned to drugs which often killed them. News articles sadden us when we read of many who are financially wealthy but are so unhappy that they even commit suicide.

Even the dictionary definition of blessed repeatedly mentions happiness. So is it possible that when the Lord gave verse 12 to Brother Malachi, God was not referring only to financial blessings, but also referring to happiness in God? "And all nations shall call you blessed" (Mal. 3:12). Might God be ok with us re-wording this scripture as, "And all nations shall call you happy?" "The joy of the Lord is your strength!" (Neh. 8:10).

Through Prophet Malachi, the Lord goes onto say that tithers shall be not only joyful, but also "a delightsome land." We already know that we are a chosen generation, a royal priesthood, an holy nation, a peculiar people (1Pet2:9). Now we learn that by simply tithing, we are a delightsome land. Psalm 37:4 says, "Delight thyself also in the LORD; and he shall give thee the desires of thine heart."

SIDEBAR: An Offering Testimony

At one point in my life, I decided to crack down on spending. I was trying to pay off some bills, so I significantly decreased my spending. While I would never "touch the tithe," I unfortunately did not give offerings for 29 THE POWER OF TITHING $$$$$ weeks. This seemed to result in not receiving any extra checks for weeks. I finally decided to pay a simple $5 offering and a check came in the mail for $369. I believe that is 74 fold? Did I do the math right? Let's see, 74 times $5=$370? That's close enough. Seventy-five fold is clearly a blessing. And that's from a simple $5 offering. What happens when the offering is $50? Better still, what if the offering is $500? Let our motive for giving an extra, special offering be simple obedience, "… Wherein have we robbed thee? In tithes AND offerings…" Malachi 3:8-10.

APPLICATION of Malachi 3:6-7

While we (people) change, and are extremely changeable, the Lord our God does not change, thank God! This is the reason that we are not destroyed, because we serve a forgiving God. We repeatedly mess up, but He repeatedly forgives us, 70 times 7, (Matt. 18:22) and more. Our ancestors through generations turned away from God on various occasions. And did not keep God's commandments and decrees periodically. But here's what God says that we can apply to our lives today: Even though our ancestors made errors with God, and we have done the same, the Lord is saying "Return to me, and I will return to you." Hopefully as you read the last sentence, you are now asking, "How do I return to God?"

In an effort to apply verse 8 to our daily lives, we should insert our names in verse 8, for example (my name being "Sarah"): "Will SARAH rob God? But SARAH asks, How do I rob you [God]? Through His Word God replies: "In tithes and offerings." Now, in order to truly apply Malachi 3 to your life, add your name to Malachi 3:10a. For example: SARAH will now "bring the *whole* tithe into the storehouse, that there may be food in SARAH'S house." Adding your name to Malachi 3:10b gives us: Now "Test me in this SARAH, says the Lord God Almighty, and see if I will not throw open the floodgates of heaven and pour out soooo much blessing that SARAH will not have room enough for it." And here's the part of this scripture that we often overlook: SARAH, "I will prevent pests from devouring your crops." In today's language that might mean: SARAH, "I will prevent job loss, household appliances from breaking down, and even a robber or thief from breaking into your home." Finally Malachi 3:12 goes onto to say: "Then all the nations will call SARAH blessed."

So please try placing your name in these sentences, do what Brother Malachi said, and see how your life changes financially. Won't He do it☺!

Jesus requires that the people of God fulfill our commitments to Him. Not only because of the Word of God, but because of our gratitude to God. We should understand that all that we have is because God gave it to us. We should be so thankful to God for all that He has done that we almost come running up to the basket to give our tithes. Recently I noticed a brother at our church who was shouting all the way down the aisle to the offering basket as he put his money in the basket, and as he returned to his seat after putting his money in the basket. I thought that the reason for this unusual activity was that he was just so full of God, and that this was the reason that he was praising God. Later God revealed to me that his shout was a shout of gratitude. This particular brother was so thankful to God that he had to shout all the way down the aisle both going to and leaving from the offering basket. This brother understood the importance of gratitude, and clearly displayed how thankful he was to God. The interesting thing is that I know for a fact that this same brother in our church often gives significant amounts in his offering, and is a consistent tither. Based on his actions, his attire, etc., I assumed that this same brother is financially blessed. God's craving is to bless His people, and to meet *all* of our needs. I wonder if some of our needs are not met because we have not committed one simple act: have we not paid our tithes?

In the lives of followers of Jesus Christ, giving takes on intense significance. For those who have received the gift of the Holy Ghost with the evidence of speaking in tongues, the Holy Spirit quickly convicts us when we do not tithe. It is then up to us to be obedient to the Holy Ghost and simply tithe, or be disobedient and not tithe.

According to Holman Bible Publishers (1988), "Levitical law required the people of Israel to give ten percent of their agricultural products plus various sacrifices and services to God" (p. 1160). In the same way, our Lord and Savior Jesus Christ now requires every blood washed believer to give 10% of our earnings, plus offerings to God. It is one thing when we do not know the Word, but once we know the Word, and know the 10% requirement, we are then obligated to pay what is due to God.

SIDEBAR: Food for Thought

*some athletes, movie stars, popular vocalists, etc. who are not church goers die with next to no money

*other stars, etc. who do not attend church live and die with huge bank accounts *is it possible that even celebrities who are not consistent members and may not even have a personal relationship with Jesus but consistently tithe are still blessed?

*Yet we who faithfully attend church every Sunday, even prayer and Bible Class during the week struggle financially? What would happen in the financial lives of believers if we added a commitment to tithing to our personal relationship with the Lord?

THE BOTTOM LINE

In summary, simply tithe. I've heard it said that the many statements in the Bible can be interpreted in different ways. While I do not agree with this statement, I can say that there are many statements in the Bible that are crystal clear with no need for interpretation, discussion, or analyzing. One of these is 1 Corinthians 6:18 which reads, "Flee fornication. Every sin that a man doeth is without the body; but he that committeth fornication sinneth against his own body." According to Dockrey, Godwin & Godwin, (2000), again fornication is sexual intercourse between two people who are not married to each other (p. 95). While in today's society the definition of "sexual intercourse" is questionable, deep in our hearts we really know the definition. So similar to simply tithing, this scripture has no need for dissection. 1 Corinthians 6:18 means simply, do not have sex if you are not married. A couple living together without having sex would be extremely tough for most people. So "shacking up" which is what they called it back in my day can only lead to fornication, which is a sin according to the Bible. In addition to fornication being a sin, statistics have shown that most couples who live together before marriage end up in divorce. So one can look at the discussion of living together this way: are you concerned about having a marriage that will last forever? Or would you prefer a short-term relationship of living together that provides unlimited sex, but ends in painful divorce after marrying but also after living together? I have not researched this next question but, I have heard that the number of divorces has significantly increased over the last 20 years. Is it possible that the number of people who live together before they marry has also significantly increased over the last 20 years? Is it also possible that there is a correlation between the increase in the number of divorces and the number of couples living together over the past 20 years? And is it also possible that the reason for the significant rise in divorces is due to the increase in couples "living in sin" or living together before marriage?

It's not rocket science: **simply do not fornicate**, and you will receive a blessed, long life of marriage. **Simply tithe**, and the Lord will pour you out a blessing that there shall not be room enough for you to receive it.

I DID NOT PLAN TO MEET JESUS

Yes, quite frankly, I did not plan to meet Jesus. Yes, I went to church as a baby through about age 13 *EVERY* Sunday with my mom. SIDEBAR: Even though our mom had not received the Holy Ghost when I was young, my sister and I were not allowed to miss church on Sunday. I did not appreciate this house rule when I was a child, but as an adult, now I understand the reason that our mother made us go. Now I wish that Momma had made us go to church even more, for example during the week. She was not perfect, no parents are perfect. But I loved our mom, and I miss her so much. She received the Holy Ghost when I was an adult. And she went to be with the Lord in 1987. I know that she is praying for me.

I knew *of* Jesus while attending church with my mom and my sister. But I did not *know* Him. I did not have a personal relationship with Him. It was only after I needed Him that I reached out to Him later in life in my early thirties. But I know that accepting the Lord as my savior was the best decision I ever made in life. Every day with Jesus is not perfect, life happens, and hardships still come. But I now have peace like never before, unlimited protection, abundant love, and most of all eternal life. And so I encourage you the reader of this book, that if you have not yet given your life to the Lord, that you please do so TODAY! Tomorrow is not promised to anyone, and while this may be a cliché, hell is a real place. But you are missing the experience of so much love from the father. Yes He loves you even now, but until you develop a relationship with Him, you are not experiencing the fullness of His love. So from your own lips right now, all you have to do is tell Jesus that you love Him, repent meaning tell the Lord that you are sorry for the sins that you committed and tell Him that you now turn away from sin, ask the Lord Jesus to forgive you of your sins, and ask Jesus to live with you forever. Please follow this up with joining a church that teaches the Word of God, which is focused on Jesus, and take the other steps outlined in Acts 2:38 to get baptized in the name of Jesus, and to receive the precious gift of the Holy Ghost.

Are you 1000% SURE that you are going to Heaven?

APPENDIX/HOMEWORK FOR THOSE WHO REEEEEALLY LOVE THE LORD:

Please read the chart below. You will see a few complaints that you may have heard about tithing. Next to the complaint, you will see a scripture to counter the complaint. Please read the scripture, tithe faithfully, then document the results of what happened in your life after you paid your tithes☺.

Complaints that I have heard from people about tithing:	SCRIPTURE SOLUTION/ COUNTER COMPLAINT/ ANTI-COMPLAINT:	Now You Document Your Results:
I just don't have the money	Numbers 18:26	
I don't have it after I pay my bills	Matthew 6:21	
I just gave $1,000 to the church	Luke 6:38	
Where in the Bible does it say, "ten percent"?	Leviticus 27:32	

Tax Savings – The Tither's Real Cost

In the example below, the Tither receives an estimated $50 monthly tax savings. Special Note for Retirees: While the Retired Tither **may** have paid tithes on the gross wages received from their employer in previous years, Jesus provides a future benefit by "pouring out a blessing that there shall not be room enough to receive" (Mal 3:10) even to the Retired Tither. (Tax rates may vary based on the financial situation of each Tither and the state in which the Tither resides).

	Person Paying "NO" Tithes	Saint "PAYING" Tithes	
Employee or Retiree Pay	2,000	2,000	
Tithes Paid	0	200	Actual cost of tithe is $150 due to $50 tax savings.
Taxable Pay	2,000	1,800	
Tax Paid (25% estimated)	500	450	
Tax Savings	0	$50	

References

Achtemeier, 1985, The HarperCollins Bible Dictionary.

Alaba, Dorothy, 1915-1990, (many prayers and teachings).

Dockrey, Godwin & Godwin, 2000, The Student Bible Dictionary.

Holman Bible Publishers, 1988, New International Version Disciple's Study Bible.

Pitts, Kevin, 2005, Preached Messages & Teachings

Showell, Franklin, 1941 – Present, (a multitude of teachings and messages).

ABOUT THE AUTHOR

Elder Sarah Ballard was born in Baltimore, Maryland and began writing at age nine. She served in the Army Reserves and Maryland Army National Guard for 21 years and was commissioned as an officer. Earning a B.S. Degree in Business Administration, Concentration, Accounting in 1986, and a Master's Degree in Business Administration (MBA) in 2016, Sarah has worked in Accounting and Human Resources for several years.

Sarah was baptized in 1991 at the First Apostolic Faith Church of Jesus Christ International, Inc., and received the gift of the Holy Ghost in November, 1992. She served in various church ministries and was consecrated as a licensed minister in 2005. Sarah was ordained as an elder in July, 2015.

While attending the New Life Discipleship Course taught by her Senior Pastor Apostle Cornelius Showell, another student asked how to learn God's purpose for your life. Apostle Showell's reply was "just ask Him." So Sarah followed Apostle Showell's instructions and asked God what did God want her to do? God's reply was "write." Sarah pursues writing out of obedience, but also uses writing as a tool to work through life's many issues as she continues to draw even closer to the Lord.

IS IT BETTER TO GIVE THAN TO RECEIVE?